SILENT CRY

RAQUEL BROWN

ISBN 979-8-89112-285-7 (Paperback)
ISBN 979-8-89112-286-4 (Digital)

Covenant Books
11661 Hwy 707
Murrells Inlet, SC 29576
www.covenantbooks.com

CHAPTER I

I can remember when I was very young, my family was not peaceful. They would fight against each other every day, and they would say terrible things to each other in front of us. As children, we were exposed to a lot of anger and violence.

The house was also open to a lot of different people, especially men. I could tell that my brother and sister were not treated fairly or equally compared to the other children in the house. My aunt would fight with her siblings, and they would even cuss and say nasty things to their own mother. It was disgraceful, but no one seemed to care.

One particular man who was at the house all the time used to sell ice cream. He was there so often that I think he eventually moved in. The house was very small, so whenever he came over, he would be in the room that I was in. This was the worst decision that anyone could have made.

The ice-cream man used to be very friendly to us. He would play with us and bring us ice cream. At first, he seemed like a nice person. But one night, I woke up to the feeling of someone touching me. I tried to hold my head up to see who it was, but I couldn't see anything. The next night, it happened again. This time, I caught the ice cream man's hands in my private area. I told him to stop, but he whispered in my ear, "If you scream or tell anyone, I'll deny it and you'll get in trouble." I was afraid of my grandmother, who was very strict. I was also afraid that if I told anyone, they wouldn't believe me. So I said nothing and just cried in silence.

The ice-cream man continued to touch me whenever he got the chance. He would stick his fingers inside my private area, and it would hurt so badly that I would bleed. I didn't know what to do, so I would just find a place to cry in silence.

I often wondered where my mother and father were. If they were around, I could have told them what the ice-cream man was doing to me, and they could have stopped him. But they weren't there, so I was all alone. I cried in silence and tried to be strong, but it was hard. I was just a young little girl, and I didn't know what to do.

CHAPTER 2

I used to wonder why we were treated differently from the rest of the cousins in the house. Why did it seem like no one cared about us? Sometimes I would cry, and no one would even ask me what was wrong. This man molested me for months, and no one even noticed. Eventually, he left the house and never came back. I didn't know what went wrong, but I was so happy. I thought that if he wasn't around, he could never touch me again, but the wounds and scars of what happened to me still hurt. I would still cry, but I never told anyone. I even had nightmares about it. When I finally told my people what he did to me, they didn't believe me, and I got beaten. It was terrifying and frustrating. But I tried to go on every day, trying not to think about it. Instead, I would just cry and ask God, "Why me?"

CHAPTER 3

I lived with my grandmother, who was a very clean woman. We had to get up early every day to do chores, such as washing dishes, cleaning the house, and carrying water. Sometimes my sister had to cook.

Life was sometimes happy, but I always wondered where my mom and dad were. My mom would come to see us from time to time, but not very often. We didn't have a phone to talk to her, so I used to cry a lot.

When I saw my other cousins with their mom and dad and the love they showed them, I wished I could have the same. I would go into the bushes to shout and cry so that no one could hear me. Then I would wipe my face, put on a smile, and pretend everything was okay.

I kept everything to myself, dying slowly and crying silently. No one knew or cared. We would wake up early to do chores, but it was mostly me and my sister who worked while the other cousins went to school.

A lot of times, we didn't get to go to school while the others always did. This made me sad because school was my only place of peace and joy. When I didn't get to go to school after working at home, I would find a place to hide and cry silently. My heart would beat so fast that I wouldn't be able to shout. I would cry because I thought it was the best thing I could do.

After crying, I would wipe my face and always try to cover it up with a smile. Maybe that's why I always have a happy smiling face today.

CHAPTER 4

I would wonder why and again ask myself, "Where are my parents?" I used to be so hardened and sad because every time I asked about my mother, all I would hear was negativity. They would speak ill of her at every chance they got, calling her names. The treatment we received was not easy to bear. Sometimes I would wonder where this hatred came from, but it seemed more like a family curse. With them fighting and hating each other every day, how could they show us love and care? For me, home was a horrible place to be, but what could I do? I was just a child.

I remember having a stepbrother who came and lived with us. He was a disabled child, and I could clearly remember how they used to hurt him so bad. I used to cry for him. My grandma used to let him kneel down on a bottle stopper. Pin close spin on his lip. She beat him mercilessly with a wire till he had bruises all over his back. She stripped him naked and let him stand outside in the rain. How heartless.

The abuse was not just from outside the home. It was also right inside, where we lived. Even my aunt was abusive. You could not learn anything from them because all that came out of their mouths were nasty words. They would laugh at everything wrong and think it was funny. They would slap me, and they did not care about my education or my future. There were always fights with the neighbors, and they would argue every chance they got. My home was not a good environment for anyone to live in. I wondered where my parents were and why they had left us in the dark. I hardly went to school, and the abuse was verbal, mental, physical, and emotional.

CHAPTER 5

Parents, please listen to your kids. Look for signs, show them love, and be there for your children. Don't allow them to end up in a situation where it's hard to change, such as committing mass shootings. Sometimes this happens because we have no one to listen to us, and we overthink a lot. So many different thoughts run through our minds, and we may act impulsively without thinking. We may even make poor decisions just to seek attention.

This is real. Show love and care. Talk to your children. Even if they are not living with you, find the time to visit. This is very important. Parents, these children need you. You have a responsibility to protect them. There are dangerous people out there waiting to abuse these kids at any chance they get. Try to protect these kids, even if they are not yours. As adults, it is our responsibility to protect all families.

Stop segregating these children; there should be no difference in treatment within the household. All kids should be loved and treated the same way. Neighbors, I'm asking you to start showing love by protecting my child. When you see them doing things they shouldn't, instead of pointing fingers and criticizing, please show more concern. Try to find out what the problem is and work together as a community to protect each other's children, no matter what race or color they are. We are one family.

CHAPTER 6

So after a few years in the same environment, nothing changed. We moved to a different city. This time, closer to the school we would be attending. I was so happy. The school was like three minutes away from our new home. I was even happier. Finally, I can get to go to school, because since money was the reason we could not attend school, now we live closer. We could walk. Finally, I start school.

The first week was okay. The second week, we missed two days. The third week, we did not attend at all. For the first month, it was just a couple of days. And after that? Sometimes weeks. We did not attend school. But bear in mind, it was just me and my sister. Every other kid in that house, they were at school every day. My heart was broken. But what can I do? I just calmed my heart, found a place, hide, and cried in silence, asking God, Why? What have I done? Why has life treated me this way? All I ever needed was to go to school. Instead, all I do is work in the house, get abused mentally, verbally, sometimes physically. So all that makes me have a heart that did not care anymore. I wouldn't even keep friends because I was ashamed of the way we live, and they would know and use it against us. So for me, it was devastating and heartbreaking growing up. It has been months and years in the same situation, and nothing has changed. Up till now, my mother and father are nowhere. They abandoned me. At the time, that's all I can think.

CHAPTER.7

After some months in our new home, we were trying to adjust to the community and the new life, even though nothing changed. It was still the same: different area but same lifestyle. After doing chores in the house, as a child, it would get boring. So we would stand at the gates, looking outside, trying to figure out what was next. As for me, I would be standing at the gate, watching other children going to and coming from school, just hoping, *When will I get to attend classes again?*

Whenever we were not doing chores at home, as girls, we would go a far distance to fetch firewood. The distance was so far away from where we lived that we would walk for hours to get there, and then the same hours to get back, with firewood on our heads. Bear in mind, my sister and I were just girls. Anything could have happened to us, but I guess no one cared. As long as we came back home with the firewood, that was all that mattered. It was so embarrassing because we had to walk past our school to get to this woodland. Whenever we tried to hide and pass the school gate so that our friends and other school children wouldn't see us and laugh, sometimes they called out to us. We would feel so bad, but what could we do?

Then after we came back, we would have to make fire, and sometimes my sister would cook dinner. But sometimes I wonder, why wouldn't they care about our education? And what would become of our lives? How can someone be this heartless and say they are your family member? I think families should love each other and protect us as children. But as for me, I never had that love or that protection. My heart aches so badly for it. And when things like that happen, you seek for attention and love elsewhere and sometimes even get caught in the trap of your abuser.

CHAPTER 8

So from time to time, I would see this gentleman talking to my grandma, mostly in the evening when he was coming from work. I came to understand that they had known each other for a long time. At the time, he was younger, maybe around twenty-six. Every day when he passed by, he would talk to me and ask me why I wasn't in school. Over time, we developed a friendship. He would offer me things like snacks and money so I could go to school. My grandma knew all of this because, after a while, she used to send me to his house to ask him for money. At this point, I began to trust him like a big brother or a father I never had. He would encourage me to stay strong and said that he would help me go to school. This made me believe in him. Until this fateful day, he asked me to come to his house to collect money so I could attend school that Monday. I was so happy, so I went to his home.

After I arrived, he asked me to come inside, but I never knew what his intention was as I trusted him like my brother, a big brother. I went inside and sat on his bed, then I turned around. When he closed the door, I asked him, "Why did you close the door?" He said he wanted to show me something, and that was when he started touching me. I tried to scream, but he covered my mouth with his hand and told me I shouldn't make any noise and threatened to hurt me if I did. So I stayed quiet. That was when he raped me. I was hurt so bad and was so heartbroken—again and again.

I never told anyone at home because of how I was treated there. I was afraid and thought that I was in trouble and was going to get beaten and talked down to. So I kept it to myself and did what I always do best: find a place and cry in silence. But that is when I figured out that nobody really loved me or cared about me. My heart became harder and harder, and the pain would not let me be. But I still tried to hide behind my smile. All that hurt and pain was killing me slowly, but I still went on, feeling a mix of hopelessness, being cast out, and worthlessness. I was only a child, but I lost all hope that anyone cared about me.

❧

CHAPTER 9

You know, as a child, we tend to think differently from an adult, especially if we don't see our parents on a regular basis. We think in our hearts and minds that we were abandoned. Only God knows how I prayed every day for my mom to come and take me away from all this. "Mom, where are you?" I questioned myself. I knew deep in my heart that my mom loved us, but I didn't know why we were not with her. And that made me feel heartbroken.

It's important to visit your kids. It's also important to let them know the reason why you won't be around for a while, just so their hearts don't stray. But after months and years of going through this, I prayed, and God finally answered my prayers. This day was the happiest day of my life. It was almost like a fairy tale when I heard my grandma say to us that we were going to live with her mother. We were finally going to move. Oh my god, the happiness I felt inside was like the day when they got the news: all the pain and hurt just disappeared. Joy was all I felt.

I couldn't wait for that day to finally have peace, love, and joy. I remember that night; I couldn't sleep. I was up waiting for morning light so we could be on our way. Because it was a long journey, all I could feel was anxiety. My heart was pumping fast. I couldn't wait for that night to end. I think it was one of the longest nights ever, but it was worth the wait. Finally, I fell asleep for a little while and went straight into a dream. I dreamt I was finally in school, having friends, but the most important part of the dream was that no one would ever hurt me again.

I woke up excited. Finally, we started getting our clothes on. I remember my grandma styled my hair with a lot of bubbles and clips. It was crowded and full, but it was beautiful. I didn't mind how tight they were because my only intention was to get to where my mom was. Finally, I was out of that house. Finally, all the abuse, the hurt, the torture, and the pain—I believed in my heart that all of this was finally going to be over and I could finally live my life as a child and enjoy my childhood. I cried, but this time it was good tears, tears of joy, tears of happiness. In no time, at last, I was home with Mommy.

❦

CHAPTER 10

At last, I was home. I got to meet my baby brother and my stepfather, as well as my beautiful mother. She was indeed a beauty to behold. Finally, I could feel at home, experiencing the love and peace I'd never felt before. After some time, we settled down. Guess what? My mom enrolled me in school. It was the happiest day of my life: I finally got to go to school and found new friends. I felt like a kid again. We were happy as a family. My stepfather was really loving and treated us well. He took care of us like the father I never had, and we were happy as a family—my brother, my sister, my mother, and my stepfather.

But the only thing I didn't like was how my mom would get upset. I used to hate it when she called us names. She was not someone easy to live with; she was very skeptical about the house and everything you touched. It would irritate her, and every time she got upset, the name-calling would begin. I don't know about my sister, but as for me, it hurt me deeply. Don't get me wrong; we were kids and sometimes we misbehaved. And I know we deserved to be disciplined, but when you put down your child by calling them all kinds of names, words cut deeper than a knife.

You must be careful with what you say to a child, especially one who has been through so much hurt, pain, and abuse. So for me, things started becoming hard again. But at least I could tolerate it because no one was abusing me, and I felt much better being with her. However, hearing those negative words would make me remember all the hurt and pain I had been through. I would always ask myself, "Why do I have to go through all this at such a young age? Why me?" Sometimes I would go to bed and find myself crying myself to sleep. It was very emotional for me. Even watching a movie and seeing kids abandoned or getting abused, I would feel it in my heart and cry because it reminded me of me.

The encouragement I must give is this: parents, stop tearing down your children with harsh words. Your tongue is like a weapon; be careful how you use it. It is soft, but it can cut deeper than a sword. All I ever needed was for my family to show me love and care. But for some reason, I never got it, and I was left wondering, "Why was it so hard to love me?"

CHAPTER II

Living with my mom was the best time of my life. I was in school every day, and I was finally enjoying myself as a child. I had new friends, and my surroundings were beautiful. But after some years, my mom and my stepfather grew apart and decided to separate. As a child, I didn't know what the problem was; the only thing I knew was that she was moving out. So she decided to move in with my grandma because we had no other place to stay. Here we go again—sigh.

She eventually moved back to my grandma's house, which wasn't a good idea, but we had no other choice. I came to realize that just as my grandma treated us abusively, she treated my mom the same way. My grandma would berate my mom every chance she got, calling her very awful names. This would make my mom cry, and my heart would break because I never liked to see it. So one night my mom decided that she was going to leave. We didn't know where we were going as we had no place to go, but she was tired of the abuse. We went to a friend's place and slept on their floor until the next day.

We then went walking, not knowing where we were going; we were just following our mother. We arrived at another lady's house, an old friend of my mother's, who offered us a place to stay until my mom could get back on her feet. At this point, we weren't in school, as my mom wasn't working and didn't have a place for us. It was a real struggle for us. We'd been through it all, but I was happy because I was with my mom. I love my mom dearly, even though she wasn't there when I needed her the most.

I don't know why she left us in the first place, but if I could make one wish, it would be that she'd never left. No matter the circumstances, I wish she had stayed back and taken care of us. Maybe then none of this pain, torture, and abuse would have ever happened. It's been a struggle, but my mom, a strong black woman, got back on her feet. She found a job and secured a place we could call home.

But one thing I can say about my family is that they have this anger problem, and I think my mother got that from my grandmother. They're quick to get angry, quick to call you names, and quick to put you down. I never liked that about her. Everything you did in the house would become a problem; you couldn't touch anything, and they didn't care about your education or future, which wasn't good. I hardly went to school anymore, and all my mom would do was verbally abuse us.

And then the pain that I had hidden resurfaced. It was as if a wound had opened up and spread all over. The pain silently crept back into my life. Why was something bad always happening wherever I turned? All I knew to do was cry in silence, thinking I'd never have a life, that nothing good could ever come from me. The harsh words they'd said to me played over and over in my head as if becoming reality. Phrases like, "You will never become anything good in life. Nothing good can ever come from you." But the most hurtful words my mother ever said to me, the words that made me lose it, were, "I don't know why you're even still living. Why don't you go to the bush and die?"

The hurt and pain I felt that day were indescribable, but I was still holding on to faith, hoping that change would come one day. No matter what I go through, something good must come. I know what they're saying is not true, but the world can be so hateful and hurtful. I always tell myself, "You can become someone, regardless of what they say. You are not the same as they are. You are a loving person with a good heart who did not get the chance to grow up as a child." My heart cries; I'm emotionally broken. Sometimes I feel like I want to die, but still no one seems to care. I have to be strong for myself. After crying, I pick up the pieces with a smile on my face and try to get over it.

Don't get me wrong, I love my mom to the moon and back. She's a good person; I just think she has an attitude problem. I believe she never tries to get to the bottom of things, never tries to solve problems or show more concern. I think she's self-centered and isn't there for her children when we need her the most. As for me, I feel rejected and abandoned by her. If only she could see deeply that we need her love and attention as our mom.

CHAPTER 12

So after some months living with my mom, we got into a conflict one day. I couldn't take the harsh words anymore. When she said she wished I'd go to the bush and die and that nothing good would come of me, my whole world shattered. Those words were so painful, I couldn't take it anymore. So I went to the river that day and decided I was going to end it all. The pain I was feeling inside was unbearable; I didn't want to live anymore. But as I sat at the riverside crying, feeling worthless and shameful, I started to shout, "I am someone! I will make it! I will not die! Rather, I'll show them that I'm a child of destiny. No matter what it takes, I will make it."

But with regret, I thought to myself, *Why was I even born? Why did I enter this world? Why has life chosen to treat me this way?* But where would I start? I was so young and had no one. Then I thought to myself, *Where is my father? Since everyone rejects me, why not try to find him?* But I had only met him once, and that was when I was about eight years old. How would I find him? *Oh Lord, please help me*, I thought. *I don't know what to do.*

So I went back home and decided I would run away. The next day, I packed my clothes and ran away. But this time, I went to my mother's sister's house. At that time, I was only fourteen years old. And can you believe it? My mother never came looking for me; I didn't see her for a very long time after that. This showed me that even she herself didn't care about me from day one. But why?

CHAPTER 13

So after I ran away, I finally reached my aunt's house. Sigh. You'd think life would be better for me? Here came my nightmare. After a week, I stopped working in the supermarket, packing bags, and then decided I wanted to go back to school. There was this training center, but I was still too young. They only accepted you if you were seventeen years old, and I was only fourteen. But I took my chance, went there, and lied about my age. They never asked for a birth certificate, so they accepted what I put on paper. After taking the tests, I passed, so I was qualified to attend class. There, I studied food and beverage.

Now I was juggling work and school at the same time. But life was hard for me because my aunt really loved money. If you could provide food and money for the house, she was your best friend. But if you couldn't, your life would be a living nightmare.

There was this guy next door whose mom had a grocery store, and at the time, the guy really liked me. So whenever his mom closed the shop, he would pack bags with foodstuffs, and when no one was looking, he would bring them over. This went on for quite a long time.

My aunt, her boyfriend, and her three kids were all living in a two-bedroom house. It was very small. With me added to that group, it was kind of difficult and cluttered, and there was hardly any privacy. Her boyfriend was one of those men who slept around with any woman; she was very insecure. With me there, he was trying to sleep with me all the time, which I refused. And because my aunt knew of his character, she was constantly accusing me of sleeping with him. But that never happened. He tried, but he failed.

I thought to myself, *Is this a generational curse? Why are all my family members the same? Careless, bitter, and all for themselves?* They didn't even think about my age or try to protect me as a child. Whenever I was unable to provide food, I would go hungry. And if I opened my mouth and complained, I would sleep outside because they would close their door and not even care about me or how I felt.

CHAPTER 14

After a while, my neighbor next door who lived in the same building noticed the way I was treated. She didn't like it because she had kids of her own, so she always tried to treat me nicely, as if I were one of her own children. Whenever they locked me outside and I had nowhere to sleep, she would sneak me into her house and wake me up early in the morning to let me out. Or whenever she had food, she would call me over, hide, and give me something to eat. She was really a great person and treated me well.

Things got so bad with my aunt that at one point she took money from a man and asked me to go with him. I was in the car, and the guy asked me if I knew why I was with him. I said no, explaining that my aunt had told me to go with him to collect something. He then told me the reason I was there: my aunt had taken money from him so that he could sleep with me. I started crying when he told me this and began explaining what I was going through. He was heartbroken to learn that I was just fourteen years old and had suffered so much. So instead of taking advantage of me, he bought me lunch, counseled me, and brought me back home. He said he was not that type of person and would never take advantage of an underage girl.

I wondered what I had done to my family. Why did they hate me so much? I don't think I was that bad a person; I don't remember doing anything to any of them. So why the bitterness and hatred toward me? It seemed they wouldn't even care about me getting hurt as long as their desires were satisfied. That's selfishness.

I was getting really tired of everyone abusing me. So when I confronted my aunt about the situation and how I was treated, she tried to beat me up. As if that weren't enough, she called her sister and told her a lot of lies about me. So both of them tried to beat me up. At this point, I was fed up; it wasn't going to go down like that. I was going to fight them with the last drop of my blood. It was really aggravating and stressful. I almost lost my mind because of these people and the way they abused me. So it wasn't going to go down like that. I fought both of them that day, and she finally threw me out.

Come to think of it, I've been through a lot of homelessness. Lord, have mercy. But now I can only laugh.

CHAPTER 15

After they threw me out, I remember my own family saying to me, "I hope you suffer. I hope you die. I will live to see you bounce around on the street, homeless, and come back to beg me for food. Then I would spit in your face and send you to eat out of the garbage." She would laugh in my face. Those were her words to me. And I remember turning around and looking at her with tears in my eyes. These were the words that I spoke: "God's got me. He will never allow that to happen to me. You will never live long enough to see me homeless, eating out of the garbage, and coming to your house to beg you. But I know you have no ambition or self-esteem. I will not wish you any bad because if I do, there will be nothing left of you. But I wish for you to live long enough to see me flourish and grow. Just remember this: I am a seed in the ground. You will never know what my destiny will be like tomorrow."

So I picked my things up off the ground, and my neighbor's sister offered me a place to stay. I decided to finish school while working. They were such nice people; they treated me well and showed me love, even though I did not know what love was. I became so attached to their family that they became a part of me; they became my family. Donna, Sabrina, Julia—how could I forget about my dear sister Laverne? I love you so much, girl. Even though you've passed away, my heart aches. I know you always wanted the best for me. All this time, as these things were happening to me, I kept writing things down. Remember I told you I was going to write a book? You are my sister, Mama—which is Miss Lydia—and Aunt Bertha. She was a very nice lady. I just wanted to tell you all how much I love and appreciate you for showing me love when my own family rejected me. Up to this day, I will always be forever grateful to you all.

CHAPTER 16

So after starting to date this guy, I realized I was trying to find love in the wrong place. As a young girl my age, I should have been more focused on school and my future. But I was forced out there to do a lot of things before my time. I was dating this guy and would often go to his house, sneaking in to spend the night. After a while, I decided I was going to look for my father, as he was the only one left who could help me. I found an old friend who knew my dad, and he gave me the address. One day, I decided to look for my father. I took a taxi, started asking questions, and gave the taxi driver the information. Finally, I found him.

I was so overwhelmed that day when I finally found my dad. He took me to my grandma's house; she was a very sweet lady. I met the rest of my brothers and sisters, and everyone seemed so kind and loving. I thought this was a new beginning for me. I didn't want to remember all the horrible things I had gone through. I was excited, overwhelmed, and happy. So when my dad tried to question me, I never told him half of what I had been through. I just pretended at the time that everything was okay and that I just wanted to meet him. But I did ask him a question I had wanted to ask for a very long time: "Why did you leave me and never look back? Did you forget about me?"

He started to explain that it was my mom and my family who had chased him away. Even then, I asked, "You never thought to look for me?" He tried to explain, offering excuses for his actions, but none of it made any sense. The fact that I found him was something I had wanted for years. So I forgave him. At the time, they were excited to see me as well. I stayed with him for four weeks, and I started to feel like a kid again. I played with my brothers and sisters. Even though my past was eating me up inside, I tried to let go and be happy.

I love my father, my brothers, and sisters. My stepmother was really nice. They all accepted me, and I became a part of their family again. So I started spending most of my time with my dad and would go back and forth to the family house—the family I met when I was living with my aunt.

CHAPTER 17

As I mentioned before, I would occasionally visit my new family and the man I had met. I would spend time with them, then return to my father. My father was showing me a lot of love and attention, which I thought was great. Perhaps he was trying to make up for the years he had missed out on.

However, as time went on, I began to notice the way he looked at me, especially when his wife and my siblings were not around. The way he touched me started to make me feel uncomfortable. It was not the way a father should touch his child. He would play with me, but then he would touch my breast as if it were an accident. Then he would apologize.

When he noticed that I knew about his behavior, I started to feel really uncomfortable being around him alone. I would constantly have flashbacks of what had happened to me in the past, and my heart would break just thinking about it. So I decided to go back to the place where I was staying.

I remember asking him for money to pay for my taxi fare, and he said it was okay until the day I was ready to go. When I reminded him, he and his wife asked me why I didn't let him touch me so he could give me more money. I was angry, disappointed, and shocked. I yelled at them and asked, "Do I have to sleep with you before you'll give me money? I'm your daughter! Are you forgetting that?" I was shocked that my father would even want to sleep with me. I knew that I had to get away from him, so I left that day and never went back.

I quickly ran out of the house and went down to my grandma. I wanted to tell her what my father said but could not find the courage. I know some people will say, "Why didn't you speak out when you have no one to stand up for you as a child and been in abuse for so long?" It became like a dark place, and you become so afraid and so ashamed to talk to anyone about the situation. And because I just met them, I did not know if they would believe me. So I spent the whole day with her, and I'd wait until it was late. I asked to sleep over. It was that night when my uncle, my father, and my brother tried to molest me in my sleep. I got up early that morning and went back out, where my father sat outside, lost, hopeless, crying. I looked at my life, wondering what to do. I lost all hope and courage, and all kinds of bad things went through my mind. At same time, my mind went blank like I was going crazy. Only God knows what I was facing. I blanked out looking at the sky, tears running down my face, wondering what my fate was going to be. I did not have a permanent home, so it was a back-and-forth. I was trying to accept fate and trying to accept what life throws at me.

CHAPTER 18

O h God, please help me. I went through depression, experienced emotional breakdowns, and felt mentally damaged. I can't even explain it; I was drained of everything in me that helped me hold on to life. Words just can't explain how I was feeling. But behind everything, I always liked to wear a smile on my face because that's what got me through my days. I never wanted anyone to know what I was going through because I was so ashamed. I kept thinking about what people would say if they knew my situation. Most people were so judgmental, and I was afraid of what they would say. So I hung in there, hoping my situation would turn around for the better.

I was at my father's house and wasn't feeling well, so I slept off. And in my sleep, I could feel someone touching all over me, so I jumped up. That was when my father tried to rape me. I cried, I screamed, but no one was there to help me. After all that, I carried so much shame, but I hid it like I always do. I felt like dying. And for a very long time, I've carried that pain in my heart, my soul.

I have sleepless nights and sad days. I cry every chance I get, crying in silence. Now I'm in my thirties and still hurt, but someday I would still like to know why all this happened to me. Did I deserve this as a young child? I used to hate remembering my life growing up because it is more painful than ever. After all that happened, I went to stay with my boyfriend for some time, hiding in his room. I couldn't live with him because he was living with his grandfather at the time. I used to hide and spend as much time as possible with him. He was the only person who made me feel loved. So at times when I wasn't there with him, I was only feeling sad. Then I would have to go back to my father's house, where he would constantly harass me, but I had no other place to go.

Around this time, I found out that I was pregnant, so I told my boyfriend. He was very happy, and I was happy at that time too. I thought having a baby might finally make me feel loved, despite my age. So my boyfriend had no choice but to tell his family, and they accepted me. His mom was a nice person. At that time, they were figuring out a place for me to stay, but until then, I was still at my father's house.

CHAPTER 19

I became really sick while being pregnant, and at that time, I was at my father's house. I remember he took me to his doctor that day for an appointment. After finishing the checkup, the doctor asked me to step out of the room while my father stayed inside. They were talking, and I was outside waiting for him. Afterward, he told me he had gotten a prescription for my medication. He said that after I took it, I would feel better. On our way home we stopped by the pharmacy, got the medication, and went home. My father told me to drink a cup of tea, take the medication, lie on my back, and cross my legs. He said I would feel much better after I woke up. I took the medication he gave me and fell asleep. I don't know how long I slept, but when I woke up, I was in so much pain. I found myself lying in a pool of blood. My father told me I was going to be okay. My brother and sister were at school at the time, and I was so weak.

There are no words that can describe what I was feeling and going through. He never took me to the hospital. I had to stand up, walk to the bathroom, and clean myself up. I couldn't even call anyone because I had no phone. I lost my baby. How wicked can he be? Crying, I wondered how my journey in this world had become so dark. Again, I questioned, "Why me?" From then on, I kept crying in silence.

When my boyfriend asked me what happened, I was so ashamed that I told him I had fallen. But deep in my heart, I knew it was the medication my father had given me. Why? I really need to know. He doesn't even realize what he's done to me. You hurt me so badly; you took away something that was a part of me, something that meant the world to me. It's as if you took my life and left me with nothing. How wicked, heartless, and selfish can one be? How could you make that decision for me? My God will judge you; my God will deal with you. Your day will come when you'll have to answer to God and explain why, as my father, you did all this to me. This pain will never go away. Sometimes I feel like taking revenge for what he did to me.

CHAPTER 20

After all these experiences, I built up hatred in my heart. I grew so cold that I stopped living. I hated everyone who came around me. I became so hateful that I would use every man who came into my life. I lost compassion; it was as if my heart had been replaced with a stone. As I aged, this coldness persisted. I couldn't feel love. I started relationships but never knew what love was. I'd say "I love you," but deep in my heart, I couldn't feel it. For years, I tried to love but couldn't find the feeling. Because of that, I hurt many good people who came my way. I would break their hearts first because I was scared mine would be broken in the end. Despite the years that passed, the hurt and pain never stopped.

I took matters into my own hands and lived life the way I thought I should—using people to get what I wanted and then discarding them. I didn't care anymore; anger had built up inside me. It felt like I was angry at the world. The least little thing would trigger me. The betrayal and pain I'd endured in life had left me heartless and uncaring. But that wasn't the end of me. God wasn't done with me yet. I had tried everything in life and failed. Family failed me, friends failed me, people I trusted failed me. But as I got older, my mindset began to shift. I told myself, "You've tried everything and failed, but there's one thing you haven't tried—you haven't tried Jesus."

So I went to church that day, and the pastor called for an altar call. I saw this as my chance. I went to the altar and gave it all to the Lord. I knelt down and cried. I was heavy, burdened, emotionally distressed, but I called out the name of Jesus. I couldn't hold back; I started shouting, "God, here I am. Help me. I need you." The pastor came over, laid hands on me, and prayed. At that moment, I felt so free, as if something had been lifted off my head. I realized that this was where I needed to be because I felt free and light. When I went home, I found myself praying and reading the Bible. I thought to myself, *What happened today? I met this man. His name is Jesus.* I used to hate myself, but when I met Him, I was on my knees and gave my life to Him. I learned how to forgive. It took time, but I learned how to love again. He made me brand-new.

I share this part of my story to say to you, girls and boys, if you're going through the same situation that I did, don't just cry in silence like me.

CHAPTER 21

Speak out now. Is anything happening to you? As I get older, I realize that keeping everything to myself was not the way. I should have found someone to talk to about everything, but it was hard because I thought I could never trust anyone. But I'm telling you, I'm encouraging you: find a friend or someone and talk about the things you're going through. Talk to your teacher, find a church and talk to your pastor. If you can't find a family member to trust, talk to friends at school or talk to your neighbor. Tell somebody about what's going on with you. Be patient. Be humble. Never think about suicide, doing drugs, or taking up guns; none of that is worth it. Trust God. There is always a light at the end of the tunnel. God will never let you down, no matter what you're going through.

Even though life has been a struggle for me, I still managed to work hard, send myself back to school, and, through all the struggles and ups and downs, obtain a certificate. I work hard; I save my money. I also bought a piece of land and built a house. And I am now married, even though it took me two failed marriages to find the right man. Even though I'm still struggling and trying to have kids, I know God will bless me. I believe help will come my way, and I have also accepted God into my life. I forgive every person who ever hurt me, and everyone I pushed away who didn't deserve it; I hope they forgive me. I was so hurt and so angry, so bitter, so confused; I couldn't understand what love meant. So whenever I met people who tried to show me love, I ended up hurting them instead. And even though I've been through so many hurts and have been neglected and pushed aside by my family, I still love them because I don't have the heart to hate them. I've learned to overcome; I've learned to forgive.

As for my family that took me in when everyone abandoned me, you showed me love. I love you guys. And as for Julie, how can I ever forget? You saved me on so many nights. In your one room with your son, you never left me out in the cold. You gave me a warm bed to sleep in. Thank you. I learned to love again; everything takes time. So you see, no matter what you go through in life, never give up. The only thing I still do sometimes is that when I remember where I'm coming from, I'm so happy I don't look like what I've been through. I lie on my bed, and I cry in silence sometimes.

CHAPTER 22

I love my family very much, and I never want to see them hurt. I would do anything to make them happy, even if it meant sacrificing my own happiness. But my family is not the type of family who knows how to show love. I don't know why I was different from them, but I always craved to hear someone say that they loved me.

I was so scared of hurting my family that I never told them anything about what was happening to me. I thought that no one would care or that they would think I was lying. I was just a child, and I didn't know how to deal with my emotions. Even though I am now far away from my family, I still love them very much. I can't find it in my heart to hate anyone, even my father who molested me. I forgive him. I cannot hate him. I hate what he did to me, but now I am older, I think differently.

I grew close to my mother and sister. My sister is now my best supporter. I can talk to her about anything, but I still never shared my whole story with her because of the shame I felt. But you know what? I am no longer ashamed. I am no longer afraid because now I want to speak out to raise awareness of what is happening in our homes and in our communities every day. Our children, our boys and girls, are being abused by the people we see every day. And it needs to stop.

One of the best things that ever happened to me was when I was seventeen years old. I met my best friend, Brenda Lynn. She became everything to me. We built a relationship where I could talk to her about anything, and I would share everything with her. She would listen; she would cry with me. That is how I built up the confidence to talk—because she was there all the time to listen. Even on the phone, we would talk. She became my strength. I love her so much, and even now, she is still my best friend. Even if we do not see each other, we talk every day. She will always remain a shoulder to lean on.

CHAPTER 23

Life is sometimes so unfair, but as a child, we don't choose life. Life chooses us. This doesn't mean that because we went through some horrible things as children, we can't have a bright future. What I'm trying to say is, no matter what you're going through or have gone through, never give up. Never turn to drugs, guns, or suicide. God can do all things if you just believe in Him and have faith. I know it's hard to have faith, especially when you've experienced many different types of abuse. It's devastating. It's horrible to know that you didn't get to live your childhood but had to grow up before your time, living each day with these horrible memories.

But remember, you're a beautiful person, inside and out. You didn't choose this part of life, so you don't have to be ashamed. Be proud of who you are. Don't blame yourself for anything that happened to you. The monsters who come into our lives—in the form of family, friends, and neighbors whom you trust and think will protect you—are most often the ones who end up hurting you. They are the ones to be blamed, not you.

I've learned a lot from my struggles growing up. It's bad enough to be rejected by your own family, but even worse to be molested by your own father. It's something you must live with every day of your life, but you know what? A lot of it made me stronger. If you just have the willpower to push on, you'll make it through. Don't give up on your dreams because of what you've been through. The sky is the limit.

Don't let anyone influence you to make you feel like you can't make it. You can. Just give life a chance. And guess what? It's always okay to cry; let it out. Don't hold it in. But after crying, wipe your tears, put a big smile on your face, and say to yourself, "Nothing is impossible through God who strengthens me."

Forgiveness is the best medicine. Once you forgive someone, you may never forget, but it can help you heal. Different people go through different situations, but no matter what your situation is, as long as you're still breathing, you can become anything. If you set your mind to it, the sky's the limit. Climb until you reach your dreams. Never give up and never feel ashamed of what you've been through.

Share your story. Try to help others who are going through the same or worse situations, because sometimes sharing your story can save someone's life or future. I have a lot more to say, but in time I will take my time and get it out. Until then, just remember: whether you're male or female, you're beautiful on the inside and out. Even if you're in a foster home and being abused, please speak out. Tell someone.

What doesn't kill you makes you stronger. Look in the mirror, put a smile on your face, and tell yourself, "I can do better. I can be better. I can be great. I can be whoever I choose to be. The sky's the limit. I will never give up. I will never be defeated. I will conquer. I will come out victorious because I am beautiful on the inside and out."

I won't let any bad energy, any negativity, or anything I've been through in my life break me down. I am not broken; I'm just bent. I will learn to stand tall. My head is above the water, and nothing can make me feel low because I am strong. I am a good person, and I will make it through. I am blessed. Nothing can ever bring me down. I will hold my head up. I will walk in my calling. I will challenge myself to be a better person.

CHAPTER 24

Some children are lucky to have good parents—both mom and dad. So when you find yourself in that situation, with parents who love you unconditionally and a family that will do anything to see you happy, to see you grow up right, and to help you get through life, you need to obey them. Don't take them for granted. You need to respect them, love them, and appreciate every bit of love that is poured out on you. Many children out there wish they were in your shoes, wishing they could have a mother and father who loved and appreciated them and took care of them. So, if you're in a home where you're receiving love and protection, don't take it for granted. Appreciate your family, listen to them, obey them, and you'll find that you'll never lose your way.

And when your mom and dad discipline you for misbehavior, don't think that it's a form of abuse. Abuse is different from discipline. Try not to follow bad company and bad ideas. Listen to your parents; the sky's the limit. Many of you grow up in good homes with parents who love you unconditionally, but because of bad company, you lose your way. Know that you can always find your way back home because it's never too late.

If you're in an abusive home, please reach out to someone. Tell them what you're going through, and one thing: never lie. Always tell the truth. Make sure that everything you say is the truth. Never give up on your dreams; dream big. If you've followed bad company that led you down the wrong path and your family is trying to help you back on your feet, don't be discouraged. It's because of the love they have for you. Accept any help to get back on your feet and appreciate them.

✧

CHAPTER 25

nd always remember: in the midst of every situation, there is a reason for everything. Our Father knows what is best for you. He will never send sunshine when He knows we need rain. But I've learned that if we put our problems in God's hands, there is nothing more we need to do; just let Him have His way. Grief and sorrow are sometimes sent into our lives not to punish us, but to help our souls grow. While we may not understand why things happen as they do, God always has a plan for us. He will never give you more than you can bear. God did not promise sunshine without rain, light without darkness, or joy without pain.

It's easy to become disheartened when nothing goes your way. It's easy to get discouraged when sickness and sorrow come your way. Let us remember that God said, "I am the way, the truth, and the life." I've learned to trust God, and I try to walk in His light. Being a Christian is not easy, but every day is a learning process. You go through trials and tribulations, but you always must pray and overcome them. I remember God gave me 1 Corinthians 13 in a dream, and from then on, I've meditated on that scripture because it talks about love. With love, you can overcome anything. That is why we must learn to forgive and love even as Christ loved us. Because even on the cross, when He was crucified, He still loved us unconditionally. He prayed for us, asking God to forgive us because we knew not what we had done. With forgiveness, love, and understanding, we can overcome any obstacle in our way.

In Psalms 35, it is said that He will never let you be ashamed; He will never allow your enemies to triumph over you. Leave all things to God, forgive, love, and free your mind. You can never change a person, but you can change yourself. You can never change the past, but you can choose your future. So don't stay on that dark path; choose the light. So now, with the power God gave me, take my hand, and let us stand, overcome, and rise together.

CHAPTER 26

This is a motto that I am encouraging you to say every day: "I am strong. I am beautiful. I can be anything I want to become in life." Look in the mirror and speak to yourself, "I am an overcomer. I forgive. I will not let negativity prevent me from achieving my goals, my aspirations in life." And always remember Colossians 3:1–17, which makes it clear to set your mind on things that are above. Until then, be encouraged. God bless you.

CHAPTER 27

Motivational speaking: I hope my journey motivates you. Thanks for reading, and remember, you can do all things through Christ who strengthens you. This is my motto.

ABOUT THE AUTHOR

Raquel plans to walk in her calling from God. Ever since she changed her life, she has worked hard, sacrificed a lot, and hoped someone will notice all her effort someday. With the support of her husband, Derrick, by her side, she believes that with God, all things are possible.